Gdansk Travel Guide

Sightseeing, Hotel, Restaurant & Shopping Highlights

Emily Sutton

Table of Contents

Gdansk

Gdansk's shipyards and maritime tradition have made it the busiest Baltic port since medieval times. From the resulting prosperity grew today's fascinating northern Polish city with its elaborate architecture and Old World charm. Formerly known as Danzig, Gdansk is of great historic significance. The start of World War Two took place in Gdansk, as did Lech Walesa's dissent against communism which ultimately resulted in the end of the Soviet rule in the 1980s.

World War Two devastated Gdansk and the entire country of Poland. It shattered the cultural heritage of the Jews in Europe and permanently changed the continent's map, and its aftermath birthed the East-West standoff history calls the Cold War.

To see where the first shots of World War Two were fired, take a boat trip to Westerplatte peninsula. For a sobering but important look at the terrors of the holocaust, book a day trip to the Stutthof Concentration camp, located about 34km outside of Gdansk. To relive the earliest blows struck against communist oppression, make your way to the Roads to Freedom permanent exhibition, located just outside Gdansk shipyard. Poland's first democratically elected president, the Solidarity leader, Lech Walesa still has his office in Gdansk, and rumor has it, that if you know the secret knock from the old days, he'll let you in for a visit.

Avid stargazers may be interested in Gdansk for another reason. The astronomer Johannes Hevellius was born in Gdansk and the science park dedicated to his heritage provides intriguing insight into his methods and discoveries. For an impression of the cutting edge of medieval technology, visit the Great Mill, which was the largest facility of its kind until World War Two, the Great Crane in the harbour or Granary Island, all of which are equally significant in terms of medieval industrialization.

The surprise of the region, lies to the northwest of Gdansk. Sopot is a resort that could be likened to the Brighton (UK) of the Baltic Sea, with its long wooden pier, promenade and fashionable main street of Monte Cassino. Another highlight are the long, unspoilt beaches of Gdynia. The Baltic Sea also yields another treasure in the form of amber, a gem that results from the fossilization of tree resin. Gdansk is often referred to as the amber capital of the world, as it is one of the best places to buy amber.

Whether you visit Gdansk to soak up some culture, history or just a bit of rare northern sunbathing, you may find yourself conquered by the vibrant and enduring spirit of this fascinating city.

Culture

From around 400 BC, the area around Gdansk was settled by Oksywska and Wielbarska tribes, who, judging by archaeological remains, may have traded with the Romans as well as the Arabs. They left graves, tools and other artefacts that were later uncovered. At a later stage, the region was conquered by the Teutonic knights and administered as a free city-state under the Hanseatic League. A significant proportion of the city's population had once been German speaking and it was better known by its German name of Danzig.

Today, about 97 percent of the country are native Polish speakers and Blacks and Asians are an extreme rarity in Poland. Although in the past, Poland had a diverse collection of ethnicities, several events of the 20th century has resulted in it presently being regarded as one of the most homogeneous nations in Europe. The Holocaust wiped out the region's Jewish population, and forced migrations under Soviet rule, saw the re-introduction of Poles from regions such as Belarus and Lithuania, while Germans were repatriated to Germany and Ukrainians compelled to move pack to the Ukraine.

Location & Orientation

Gdansk is located on the Baltic sea, near the mouth of the Motlawa River. It is the capital of the region Pomerania and makes up part of an urban area known as the Tri-city, along with nearby Sopot and Gdynia. It is Poland's most prominent sea port and also a popular summer destination for Polish holidaymakers. It is the 6th largest city in Poland.

The Gdansk Lech Walesa Airport is conveniently located to serve the Tri-City area of Gdansk, Sopot and Gdynia. It is 12km from Gdansk and 10km from Sopot. As an international airport, it offers connections to Berlin, Amsterdam, Frankfurt, Munich, Warsaw, Paris, London, Barcelona, Oslo and Copenhagen. Gdansk is also connected by rail to various cities in Poland and across Europe. There is a regular train service from Gdansk to Sopot and Gdynia. A ferry service links Gdansk with Gdynia. There are ferries between Gdansk and Nynashamn in Sweden.

The inner city has a fairly cheap bus and tram system, with most routes costing only 3zl. It may be beneficial for visitors to get a Tourist Card from one of the city's information outlets. This qualifies you for numerous discounts and free offers at museums, tourist attractions, as well as on the metropolitan transport network of Gdansk. The main artery of the Old Town is Dluga or Long Street.

Climate & When to Visit

Gdansk enjoys a temperate climate with hot summers and cold winters. Light rainfall can occur during the warmer months, with August and September generally being the wettest period. Snowfall can be expected, especially during January and February.

The warmest months are July and August, when day averages can settle around 21 degrees Celsius, while night averages of 11 degrees Celsius are experienced, but temperatures could rise as high as 30 degrees Celsius. In June, temperatures fluctuate between highs of 18 degrees Celsius and lows of 9 degrees Celsius. May and September are a little cooler with day averages between 15 and 16 degrees and night temperatures of between 5 and 8 degrees Celsius. April and October see figures of around 11 degrees Celsius during the day and night averages between 2 and 5 degrees Celsius.

During the winter months, you can expect temperatures to barely move between frigid day averages between 4 and 0 degrees Celsius and night averages between -1 and -5 degrees Celsius, but temperatures could drop as low as 20 degrees Celsius.

Sightseeing Highlights

Royal Way

Droga Krolewska or the Royal Way was a ceremonial route of about 500m travelled by the Polish kings on official visits to Gdansk. The city was entered through the moated Brama Wyżynna or Upland Gate. From here, the monarch would reach the Złota Brama or Golden Gate and ride through Ulica Dluga (Long Street) and Dlugi Targ (Long Market Street) towards Zielona Brama or the Green Gate. Gdansk was a good source of tax revenue and the citizens of Gdansk would petition the king to shield their interests and rights from Prussian demands.

Brama Wyżynna/Upland Gate

The Upland Gate marked the starting point of the Royal Way. Here, the king was officially welcomed and presented with the keys to the city. Originally the gate was surrounded by a moat and flanked by an earthen wall of matching height. Today it is free standing. The metal pulleys once used to manipulate a drawbridge are still visible and the design incorporates the heraldic emblems of Gdansk, Prussia and Poland. The gate dates back to the 16th century and remains an impressive sight. It now houses a tourist information point.

Zlota Brama/Golden Gate

Dating back to around 1612, the style of the Golden Gate was strongly influenced by the Italian Renaissance. It replaced an older Gothic style gate from the 13th century. Its creator, Abraham van den Blocke, was educated in the Netherlands, but lived in Gdansk. The design is topped by eight statues. The four facing towards Upland Gate represent Peace, Freedom, Wealth and Fame, while the four facing Dluga symbolize Concord, Justice, Piety, and Reason. A Latin inscription states *Small states grow in harmony, large states fall in discord*. The Gate was rebuilt in 1957, after damage from World War Two.

The Golden Gate is the second portal of the Royal Way. Through it, you gain entry to Dluga street. The view is quite impressive and includes the Old Town Hall.

Brama Zielona/Green Gate

Długi Targ 24, Gdansk
Tel: (+48) 58 307 59 12 ext. 102
http://www.muzeum.narodowe.gda.pl/

The Green Gate marks the end point of the Royal Way. It was built between 1568 and 1571 to serve as a residence for the use of visiting Polish kings. Its design, which features a four arched gate, was inspired by Flemish architecture. Today, the Green Gate houses collections of the National Museum of Gdansk. It is sometimes used for special exhibitions. Lech Walesa also has his office within the building.

Artus Court

Long Market 43-44, Gdansk
Tel: +48 58 767 91 80
http://www.mhmg.pl/

It must have been quite something to see Artus Court in its heyday. Wealthy merchants and aristocrats dined on lavish feasts, while enjoying performances from a variety of entertainers ranging from singers and musicians to dancers and jugglers. There was no actual talk of business, though. That was delegated to the yard outside. Only the elite were allowed entry.

Artus Court was built between 1348 and 1350. The name "curia regis Artus" or the Court of King Arthur alludes to the incredible impact the legend of King Arthur had on popular culture in the Middle Ages and the Saint George Brotherhood, an elite grouping of knights played an important role in its establishment. The building served as a gathering place for wealthy merchants and dignitaries, where important news was often exchanged.

Archaeological evidence uncovered in the 1990s suggests that it burnt down in 1476 and was rebuilt around 1479. The impressive facade was the work of Abraham van der Blocke. A Baroque staircase dates back to the 18th century, as does various paintings and sculptures. Another interesting feature is an 11m furnace dating back to the 1500s. This is covered with over 500 individually crafted tiles.

Presently, Artus Court houses a collection of Gdansk History Museum. It is open to the public. Admission is 10/5zł, but Tuesdays are free.

Great Mill

ul. Wielkie Młyny 16, Gdansk
Tel: 58 305-24-05
http://www.wielkimlyn.gda.pl/

The Great Mill dates back to 1350 when it was constructed by the Teutonic knights. Its 18 wheels were initially powered by slaves, but this changed around 1356, when the Radunia Canal was built. The mill represented the largest industrial complex of medieval Europe. In recent years it has been rebuilt into a shopping center, although the old equipment is still on display.

Bazylika Mariacka/St Mary's Church

ul. Podkramarska 5, Gdansk
Tel: (+48) 58 301 39 82
http://www.bazylikamariacka.pl/

St Mary's Church is the largest brick built church in the world. It can accommodate up to 25,000 worshippers and its towers and spires can be seen from various parts of the city. For a panoramic overview of Gdansk, climb the 408 steps to the top of the church.

St Mary's has a few interesting features. The astronomical clock dates back to 1464. It includes a representation of moon phases, the zodiac and a saint's calendar. There are various examples of beautiful stained glass art, as well as paintings by Hans Memling, including a replica of *The Last Judgement*, a painting seized as loot by the privateer Paul Beneke, in allegiance with the Hanseatic League and various sculptures of note. The pulpit is a fine example of Baroque design and the vault houses over 300 tombs. Other features of note include the black Madonna, the high altar and the huge organ. During World War Two, the church suffered some damage and it provided sanctuary to Solidarity members during the early 1980s. A small donation is levied. Ascending the tower costs 5zl.

Roads to Freedom Exhibition

24 Waly Piastowskie St., Gdansk 80-855
Tel: (+48) 58 308 44 28
http://www.ecs.gda.pl/

Gdansk shipyard is a location of huge historical significance, as it set the scene for a key struggle between the dockworkers of Gdansk and the Soviet Union. The action provided an early spark to the fire of dissent that ultimately dismantled communism in Eastern Europe. The details of this important event and the social circumstances that led to it, are well presented at the Roads to Freedom Exhibition, which can be found near the entrance to the old Lenin Shipyard, now Gdansk shipyard.

Different rooms are devoted to different stages of the struggle towards liberation for the Polish people. One diorama graphically depicts a typical communist style grocery store where the shelves are empty except for containers of vinegar and mustard. Another display features the demands of the striking Solidarity workers in 1980, hand-written on the original plywood board used. There is an old copy machine, as well as a public phone booth, with an out-of-order sign attached.

The exhibition is informative, using various media such as photographs and film to represent life in communist Poland. It chronicles the period from the end of World War Two to 1989 and presents a detailed timeline of the history of the Solidarity Movement. Most of the descriptions are subtitled in English and an audio guide is also available. The exhibition is closed on Mondays.

Westerplatte Peninsula

ul. Sucharskiego, Gdansk

During the 19th century, Westerplatte was a pleasant resort with its own beach area, a number of health spas and a forest park. It was connected to the mainland only via a slim isthmus. The creation of the Free city of Danzig in the aftermath of World War One, gave the region considerable strategic significance, and from 1925, it hosted a small military presence.

On the 1st of September 1939, Polish vigilance was tested when an unprovoked volley of canon fire erupted from the German battleship *Schleswig-Holstein*, which had been in the vicinity of Gdansk (or Danzig, as it was then known) at the time. Polish forces held out against the German attack for seven days, but injuries and a shortage of necessary food, water, ammunition and medical supplies led to their surrender on the 7th of September. This marked the start of the German occupation of Poland.

Today, Westerplatte is a memorial site. Set against a beautiful environment of natural vegetation, the location includes a 25m memorial, the ruins of guard houses and barracks and a museum, which can be found inside Guardhouse number 1. The memorial, which is named *Heroes of Westerplatte*, is composed of 236 granite blocks. Designed by Adam Haupt and Franciszek Duszenko, it was installed in 1966. Two shells from the battleship *Schleswig-Holstein* are mounted against the entrance to the site and there is a permanent outdoor exhibition entitled *Westerplatte: Spa-Bastion-Symbol*. The displays reflect some of the pre-war life of Westerplatte. One fun way to get to the Westplatte is via the *Black Pearl* pirate ship, which costs 25zl.

Stutthof Concentration Camp

Ul. Muzealna, Sztutowo 82-110
Tel: +48 (55) 47 8353

Completed on the 2nd of September 1939, shortly after the invasion of Poland commenced, Stutthof was the first concentration camp built outside the pre-war boundaries of Germany. It was ironically also the very last one to be liberated. During its years of operation, the facility claimed the lives of over 85,000 inmates. The first 150 inmates arrived on the first day, and by the 15th of September 1939, they already numbered 6000. Ultimately, what started out as a modest camp made up of eight barracks, expanded to a complex that housed up to 110,000 people, from 25 nationalities. These included Jews, Gypsies, Czechs, Latvians, Austrians, Ukrainians, English, Spanish, Dutch and of course Poles.

Visitors to Stutthof can view the original gate, the gas chamber and the original box carts in which prisoners were transported. There is for example a mound made up of confiscated shoes, and black and photographs document events such as the arrival of the first prisoners and a visit from Heinrich Himmler. Information is given in both English and Polish. There is also a memorial to the victims. Prepare for a highly emotional encounter with human history at its darkest. Admission is free. The Stutthof Concentration Camp is accessible from Gdansk by bus.

Centrum Hewelianum

ul. Gradowa 6, Gdansk
Tel: (+48) 58 742 33 52
http://www.hewelianum.pl/

The Polish astronomer Johannes Hevelius was born in Gdansk in 1611. By profession, Hevellius brewed beer, but he also served as town councillor and eventually mayor of Gdansk, but that is not what history remembers him for.

Hevelius advanced the study of the heavens by using flatter lenses for his telescope. This provided a clearer image of the stars. As a result, he discovered four comets and identified several constellations, but he is perhaps best remembered as the first to chart a detailed topography of the moon. His second wife, Elisabeth shared his interest in astronomy and published two of his books posthumously. She can be regarded as the first female astronomer.

Fort Grodzisko, which dates back to the era of Napoleon, houses a science park and museum dedicated to honoring the work of Johannes Hevelius. Using modern audio-visual equipment and interactive displays, the facility demonstrates the legacy we owe to the studies of Hevelius. There are activities geared towards various age groups. Admission is 8/6zł.

Maritime Museum of Gdansk

ul. Ołowianka 9-13, Gdansk
Tel: (+48) 58 301 86 11

The Maritime Museum of Gdansk is one of the biggest museums in Europe and showcases a proud tradition of maritime trade and technology, which goes back several centuries. The concept of a maritime museum was first introduced around 1958 and became a reality in October of 1960. Over time, it expanded to include buildings and structures on both sides of the river. A museum ferry, the "Motlawa" connects various sections of the museum.

On the right bank, you will find a series of reconstructed granaries, some dating back to the 15th century. The granaries were a source of considerable wealth to the port of Gdansk. During the 14th century, there were over 300 of them and they were serviced by up to 200 ships a day.

The museum complex includes a medieval port crane and the museum ship Soldek, the first steamship constructed in Gdansk after World War Two. The Soldek provides a living presentation of life at sea and includes a close encounter with the ship's engine room, bridge and cabins. A new facility on the same side of the river as the crane focusses on the cultures of maritime activity around the world. A permanent exhibition entitled *People, Ships, Boats* displays various styles of boats and ships, as used by different people around the world. It also features treasure salvaged from various shipwrecks. A restaurant on the 4th floor offers great views of the river below.

The main museum displays an abundance of informative material, which is available in English. It includes a large collection of ship models, oil paintings depicting Poland's naval history and items of weaponry such as cannons and harpoon guns. This section is located within three granaries, dating back to the Renaissance. Admission is 18zl, which includes admission to the museum, the SS Soldek, a ferry ride and access to the big crane. Expect to spend at least a few hours exploring this fascinating view on the past.

Big Crane

Ul Szeroka

The crane of Gdansk harbour is first referred to around 1367. It was used not only to load cargo, but also to position the masts of ships being built or repaired. Additionally, it served as a gate or access point and could even be utilized for defence purposes. It was the biggest structure of its kind in Europe. The original crane was made of wood, but this burnt down in 1442. It was rebuilt and the new design resembled the crane, as it can be viewed today. It worked with two hidden wheels near the center of the structure and could lift goods of up to 4 tonnes. The crane remained in use until the 19th century, but suffered considerable damage during World War Two.

The reconstructed crane was donated to the Maritime museum. It houses a collection of exhibits dedicated to port activities from the 1500s to 1700s. There are also models of various lighthouses and visitors can get a close view on the cogs inside.

Pomnik Poległych Stoczniowców/Monument to the Fallen Shipyard Workers

Pl. Solidarności, Gdansk

The Monument to the Fallen Shipyard Workers was created in 1980 to remember the 42 casualties of protests that were sparked in 1970 by sudden and sharp increases in food prices. Located at Gate 2 of Gdansk Shipyard, where the first victims fell, the memorial features a steel sculpture 42m high and weighing 139 tonnes.

Ratusz Starego Miasta/Old Town Hall

ul. Korzenna 33/35, Gdansk
Tel: (+48) 58 301 10 51
http://www.nck.org.pl/

There are two town halls in Gdansk, both dating back to the 14th century, when they represented the interests of two separate town councils. The front garden of the Old Town hall features a statue of Johann Hevelius, the famous astronomer, who was once a town councillor. It is one of the few buildings that escaped World War Two with minimal damage. Today, the Old Town Hall periodically hosts concerts and includes a book shop and a restaurant. It is open to the public.

The Main Town Hall is located on Ulica Dluga or Long Street and now houses the History Museum. It features exhibits ranging from art to weapons and other historically significant artefacts.

Museum of Amber

Targ Węglowy 26, 80-001 Gdansk
Tel: +48 58 301 47 33

Amber is sometimes referred to as Northern gold or Baltic gold. This is because approximately 75 percent of the world's amber is mined in Northern Poland. Amber is a fossilized form of tree resin and it occurs in an unbelievable 300 different shades.

At the Museum of Amber, which is housed in the medieval Gateway Fortified Complex, you can see the variety of tints and uses for this fascinating substance. Some of the items on display include chandeliers, clocks, an unfinished church altar and a Fender electric guitar, made of a combination of amber and maple wood. On the second floor of the building, you can see a detailed display that depicts how amber is formed. The mezzanine floor includes samples of the work of various contemporary creators of amber jewellery. The museum also has a wide collection of specimens that feature interesting inclusions, ranging from pieces of plant matter or insects, to Gierlowska's lizard, a nugget that contains a very recognizable portion of a lizard within. Admission is 5zl, while a combination ticket that includes a visit to the prison tower is 10zl. Tuesdays are free.

Sopot

Once a humble fishing village, the development of Sopot as health resort began when Jean Haffner, a French army doctor with Napoleon's forces, decided to settle down here. The high concentrations of iodine that occurs naturally in the air around Sopot, are known to have health benefits, but Haffner added baths and spas, which soon became fashionable. Road and rail connections were established, a casino was built and tennis courts were laid out. The promenade is a popular area and the main commercial strip is Monte Cassino street, which features some interesting examples of Art Nouveau architecture, including the highly unusual Krzywy Domek or Crooked House, which was built in 2004.

The beach at Sopot features a long expanse of fine white sand. It offers great views of the Baltic sea and the Orlowo headland. While the sea is cold, conditions are ideal for windsurfing. There are also facilities for jet skiing and paragliding and bike rentals can be organized. The beach area is flanked by sections of the Trójmiejski Park Krajobrazowy or Tricity Landscape Park, an attractive woodland region that offers plenty of opportunity for strolling or cycling.

The Sopot Aqua park features a variety of attractions, ranging from swimming pools, a wild river ride, cascades, water grottoes and water massages. The water is heated and the facility has a bar and restaurant. Your tab of usage is linked to an electronic wristband system. The Sopot Hippodrome is used for horse racing, festivals, concerts and other events. The Museum of Sopot, is located at 8 Poniatowski Street and offers a rare glimpse into the household of the early 20th century merchant Ernst Claaszen. It includes paintings, furniture, photographs and post cards. Admission is free.

Gdynia

Gdynia forms part of the extended urban sprawl known as the Tricity, which includes Gdansk, Sopot and Gdynia. The city has a long coastline with several beaches, each unique in its appeal. The city beach, Plaza Miejska, is perhaps the best developed with its marina and promenade area.

Plaza w Orlowie offers great views of the nearby Orlowo cliffs, while Osada Rybacka is an unspoilt terrain with plenty of props left over from its use as a fisherman's beach. Two museum ships are anchored in Gdynia harbour. They are the ORP Blyskawica, a destroyer from the Polish navy and the Tall ship, Dar Pomorza. Gdynia also has an aquarium.

Recommendations for the Budget Traveller

Places to Stay

Gotyk House

Mariacka 1, Stare Miasto, Gdansk 80-833
Tel: +48 58 301 85 67
http://www.gotykhouse.eu/en/

Gotyk House is centrally located on the attractive Mariacka street in the Old Town, in a building which allegedly dates back to 1450. This modest hotel is believed to be connected with Anna Schilling, a sweetheart of the astronomer, Copernicus and there is a museum of sorts located in the basement as well as what is described as the oldest gingerbread shop in Gdansk.

The structure is compact and there is no elevator, but rooms are clean and spotlessly maintained. Each room has its own interior theme and has free Wi-Fi coverage. The bathroom facilities are quite modern and staff are described as friendly. Accommodation begins at $69 (zl200) for a single room and includes breakfast.

La Petite Hotel

Na Zboczu 39, Gdansk 80-110
Tel: +48 58 320 76 26
http://www.lapetite.pl/

La Petite Hotel is centrally located near the Old Town of Gdansk and many of its tourist attractions. It is a small hotel, which offers friendly service. The breakfast room doubles as a conference room. Rooms are spacious and modern and include satellite TV, radio, fully equipped bathroom facilities and free high-speed internet. Accommodation begins at 190zl. ($59). A buffet breakfast is served.

Hotel Focus Gdansk

ul. Elblaska 85, Gdansk 80-718
Tel: +48 58 350 08 01
http://www.focushotels.pl/

Hotel Focus in Gdansk is located near the city center and has plenty to offer. The hotel has a fitness center, sauna, business center, bar/lounge and restaurant.

The decor is modern and functional and staff are described as friendly and helpful. Rooms include air-conditioning, television, a bathroom with shower or tub, coffee and tea making facilities and free Wi-Fi internet. There is a breakfast buffet. Accommodation begins at 149zl ($46).

Akme Villa

st. Drwecka 1, Gdansk 80-110
Tel: +48 58 302 40 21
http://akme.gda.pl/

Akme Villa is a modest establishment that offers friendly service and accommodation that is comfortable and well-maintained. There is no bar, but the lobby has a fridge that is stocked with soft drinks and bottles of water. All rooms include television, shower facilities, a hairdryer and free Wi-Fi internet. Free parking is also available. Accommodation ranges between 140zl ($44) and 210zl ($66) and includes breakfast.

Scandic Hotel

Podwale Grodzkie 9, 80-895 Gdansk
Tel: (+48) 58 3006000
http://www.scandichotels.com/Hotels/Poland/Gdansk/Scandic-Gdansk/

The Scandic Hotel in Gdansk is centrally located near the Old Town and many of its attractions.

The hotel has a fitness center, games room, spa, steam baths, restaurant, bar and business center. Bicycle rentals can be organized from reception, which is manned 24 hours. Rooms include television, a safe deposit box, hairdryer, iron, en suite bathroom and coffee and tea making facilities and free Wi-Fi internet. Accommodation begins at 278zl ($85.50).

Places to Eat & Drink

Bar Mleczny Neptun

ul. Długa 33/34, Gdansk
Tel: (+48) 58 301 49 88
http://www.barneptun.pl/index.php?lang=en

At the height of communism, milk bars provided cheap, state-subsidized food for the masses. To get some insight into that era, visit Bar Mleczny Neptun, a favorite of pensioners, blue collar workers and backpackers. Once inside, grab yourself a tray and take your pick of what is available in the canteen. While the variety can diminish towards the end of the day, you can expect freshly cooked, basic fare such as pork chops and mashed cabbage, goulash, beef roulade, liver, hamburger, sausage, fruit soup, chicken soup and borscht. There can be up to twelve different soups, plus a good selection of vegetarian, meat and fish dishes. The menu is in Polish only, but you can probably get by with gestures towards the dish of your choice.

There is a breakfast and dessert menu as well. Bar Mleczny Neptun has indoor and outdoor seating. Expect to pay around $4 (12.65zl) to $5 (15.90zl) for a generously portioned plate of food and more. Wi-Fi is also available.

Bar Mleczny Syrena

Grunwaldzka 71, Gdansk

As a carry-over from communist austerity, the remaining milk bars of Poland offer unbeatable value for money, serving home cooked food in a canteen-style environment. At Bar Mleczny Syrena, you can load up your tray with typical Polish fare such as pierogi and other filling choices such as cutlets, schnitzels, bigos and a selection of vegetarian options. Expect to pay between 4zl and 12zl for your plate of food.

Pierogarnia u Dzika

ul. Piwna 59/60, Gdansk
Tel: +48 58 305 26 76

The house speciality at Pierogarnia u Dzika is a traditional Polish dish, Pierogi - a dumpling that can be served with a variety of fillings. The usual combination is potato and white cheese, but the restaurant offers a great selection of other alternatives, including wild mushroom and spinach, pork and game. Other dishes include chicken, soup, salads, herring and sour cream as well as duck breast.

The food is freshly prepared and service is quick. A terraced area provides outside dining. For 26zl, you can enjoy a Pierogi combo of four, with the choice of two different fillings. Pierogarnia u Dzika has an attractive location and offers great ambiance.

Original Burger

Dluga 47-49, Gdansk 80-831
Tel: (+48) 666 847 077

As the name implies, Original Burger is basically a burger joint, featuring wide armchairs and a collection of retro movie posters in the interior. Some of the options include the chicken farmer burger, the cod burger, the cheese and bacon burger, the wild hog and black pudding burger, the Mexican burger and the veggie burger. Besides French fries, the side items include potato salad, coleslaw and onion rings. Portions are described as generous and the serving staff do speak English. Some of the beverages available include orange juice, coffee, tea and Polish draught beer. Expect to pay around 20zl for a burger of your choice. A portion of French fries cost 7.50zl.

Tekstylia

Szeroka 121-122, 80-835 Gdansk
Tel: +48 58 304 77 63
http://www.facebook.com/tekstylia

Tekstylia is located within an old textile factory that has been revamped. Some of the breakfast options include scrambled eggs, pancakes with orange syrup and ice cream and for the super-hungry, the three-egg omelette. Other dishes served feature grilled chicken breast, salmon and shrimp tagliatelle, schnitzel, fish soup and pierogi with duck. The coffees are excellent and, as a novelty, teas are named after Winnie the Pooh characters. You can also quench your thirst with lemonade, smoothies or fruity sangria. Menus are available in English. Expect to pay between 21zl and 34zl per person.

Places to Shop

Where to Buy Amber

Poland is well known for its amber, which is often referred to as Baltic gold. There are stalls and shops selling amber throughout the Tri-city, but Mariacka Street in Gdansk is a particularly good place to browse, as there are numerous shops selling a large variety of amber items.

Along Dluga you will also find a number of shops selling amber. The amber artist Lucjan Myrta has a workshop at Gallery Sopot (Tel: +48 601 786 886) in Sopot. He is one of Poland's most renowned crafters of amber.

To educate yourself on the quality of amber, visit the Museum of Amber, which features detailed displays on different types of amber. There is also an outlet of Galeria S&A within the Museum. Galeria S&A has another shop on Mariacka 36. They trade under certificate from the International Amber Association. Bernstein at Dugi Targ 22/23 in Gdansk represents three generations of experience working amber. Here you can get a quick tutorial in how to recognize an authentic piece of amber and, do browse through the goods on display while you are at it. When buying ask for an amber passport as certificate of authenticity.

You may be interested in trying a typically Polish novelty - drinking amber. While this may sound disrespectful, you could buy an unpolished piece of amber from one of the stalls on Mariacka street and leave it in pure vodka. It dissolves within about 10 days, at which time you should have a truly exotic tipple, said to cure headaches. The pre-bottled amber in vodka, can be bought from Brama Mariacka at Mariacka 25/26 in Gdansk.

Cepelia

47 Dluga, Gdansk
Tel: (+48) 58 301 27 01

A great place to browse for souvenirs and gifts, is Cepelia, a Polish organization with outlets across the country. It was create to promote and encourage Polish arts and crafts. Cepelia has branches all over Poland and sells a wide selection of traditional Polish crafts such as hand-made linen table cloths, woollen sweaters, hand-carved wooden boxes, porcelain and dolls wearing folk costume. They also sell Polish pottery and ceramics. In Gdansk, Cepelia has outlets at Dluga 47, Jana Kochanowskiego 41 and Jagiellonska 10H. Gdynia has its own Cepelia shop at 2/4 ul. Świętojańska.

Galeria Sztuki Kaszubskiej (Kashubian Art Gallery)

ul. Św. Ducha 48, Gdańsk
Tel: (+48) 503 00 59 78
http://www.gskart.pl/

The Kashubians are a very small ethnic minority in Poland, representing only a few thousand of the population, but they produce beautiful folk art, especially embroidery. Each of the colors used have specific symbolic meanings.

The Kashubian Art Gallery specializes in a wide variety of items, including bibs, specs cases, bookmarks, towels and handkerchiefs. In the Polish china section, you will find tea pots, tea cups and saucers. There are folk sculptures in both devotional and secular themes and also a range of linen clothing.

Goldwasser

Ul. Dlugie Pobreze 22, Gdansk
Tel: (+48) 58 301 88 78
http://www.goldwasser.pl

An alcoholic beverage that is unique to Gdansk is Goldwasser vodka. It dates back at least to the late 16th century and is said to be the creation of Ambrose Vermollen, a Dutch immigrant to the city Gdansk. The sweet syrupy taste is the result of a blend of about 20 herbs and roots, but one element makes this drink truly unusual - the 23 gold flecks found in each bottle. There are several legends associated with this occurrence, mostly linked to the tradition of tossing coins into the Neptune fountain for luck. Gift sets of Goldwasser can be bought at the Goldwasser restaurant.

Shopping in Gdynia & Sopot

The main shopping streets in Gdynia are Świętojańska and Starowiejska. Ul. Świętojańska boasts about 2km worth of shops, restaurants and bars.

For a huge range of amber items, set in gold or silver, visit the Silver and Amber Galaria Nova, at ul. 10 Lutego 11. As they are associated with a number of highly rated designers, you can be assured of both quality and variety. Desa at ul. Abrahama 54, sells art and antiques.

There is a large market, Hala Targowa, at ul. Wojta Radtkego 36, that sells fresh produce and fish, as well as some flea market items. On the other hand, if you are looking for malls, visit Klif at Al. Zwycięstwa 256. This is the original Tricity mall, with over 150 shops, many of them outlets of well-known international names. The mall is located right by Gdynia Orłowo train station. Another shopping mall worth visiting is Gemini at ul. Waszyngtona 21. Besides shops and restaurants, there is a flea market section where you can buy hand made art and craft items.

The main shopping street in Sopot is Monte Cassino, a long pedestrianized strip that leads to the pier. A street market trades on Tuesdays and Fridays at Sopot Wyścigi Station. Here you can buy antiques, jewellery and clothing, as well as fresh produce.

Printed in Great Britain
by Amazon

59115872R00030